PLEAS

Help for a Dog with Separa...

Tonya Wilhelm

PLEASE STAY
Help for a Dog with Separation Anxiety

Copyright © 2015 Tonya Wilhelm

Editor Janet Carlson

Because of the dynamic nature of the Internet, any web addresses or links contained in this book may have changed since publication and may no longer be valid.

ISBN-13: 978-1506180618

Printed in the United States of America

Dedication and words of thanks.......

This booklet is dedicated to all of the families and their dogs who suffer through separation anxiety. I too have lived through the pain and stress of having a dog that panics when a loved one leaves. This booklet is to help those families and give them hope.

I want to extend a big thank you to my editor, Janet Carlson, who has been by my side throughout this booklet. Without you, my message would be much rougher around the edges.

Theo

Contents

Introduction

The human – canine bond, if you know dog parents, or professionals who work with animals, you have probably heard countless comments about the special bond they share with their dog. Yes, it's true; we love our animals to pieces and it seems like we can never get enough of them. Dogs are part of our daily lives, whether in our homes or through social media, they are in our schools, airports, and hospitals. Dogs are indeed everywhere and for that, I am extremely grateful.

As a dog Mom, and outright dog fanatic, there isn't anything I would rather do than spend time with my canine companion and I am sure you feel the same way. Studies have shown that the feeling is mutual from our dogs; they are social creatures who thrive on human companionship. Unfortunately, there are times when their desire to be with us can lead to unhealthy behavioral problems and distress. This type of stress in dogs is commonly referred to as separation anxiety.

Separation anxiety in dogs is a condition where a dog experiences distress when left alone.

According to one study[1] it is estimated that 20-40% of dogs seen by animal behavior practices in North America suffer from separation anxiety. **Most dogs with separation anxiety usually begin to show signs of distress when the owners are starting their departure routine**. A dog can display his feelings of distress in many different ways, one being a full blown panic attack where the dog can be destructive to themselves and to objects around them. Other behaviors your dog might use to express his feelings of stress can include elimination, chewing walls and furniture, shaking, and drooling excessively. Dogs have even been known go as far as to jump through windows.

Separation anxiety in dogs can be brought on by a variety of reasons. The addition of a new family member, such as a baby or a pet, is a very common trigger. Other events that may activate your dog's anxiety can include the loss of a family member, the loss of a pet or a traumatic event while left alone such as during a thunderstorm, fire, or home robbery. Sometimes actions that seem perfectly normal to you can trigger anxiety behaviors in your dog. For example, being left at a boarding kennel, a shelter, a veterinary facility or even a simple change in the household schedules can raise the dogs stress level. **Once you have finished reading this book it will be clear to you that the main reason for separation anxiety in dogs is the lack of a prevention program.**

A dog's personality can play a big role in how they respond to the above mentioned situations. If a dog is clingy, fearful, and nervous or lacks self-confidence, they can be more prone to develop behavioral problems.

Separation anxiety can happen at any time in a dog's life but tends to develop in dogs under two years of age. If a dog develops separation anxiety in their middle, or senior years, you should talk to your veterinarian to rule out cognition dysfunction, hypothyroid disease, arthritis, blindness or deafness. Of course, any dog that develops a behavioral condition should always see their veterinarian for a full medical work up. Pain has a way of surfacing through behavioral problems in animals.

Unfortunately, I know about these risk factors oh too well. I had a wonderful golden retriever named Theo that could check off almost everything on this list. Theo and his two brothers were found as strays when they were just three months old. The animal shelter kept them for a week hoping that their previous owners would come looking for them. At the time I was on staff as a dog trainer at an assistance dog organization so when the original owners did not come forward we took all three puppies into our program. I adopted Theo and over the course of his first year he started to show signs of anxiety and low self-confidence. Around one year of age, Theo was left at home alone during a big thunderstorm and from that point forward he developed separation anxiety and storm phobia. Theo and I experienced a roller coaster of ups and downs with his anxieties. I was able to cure his separation anxiety through the fall and winter months but when spring and summer storms rolled around we were back to square one. Theo had developed an intense fear of storms that would always send him into a panic; therefore triggering his separation anxiety every spring.

Does My Dog Have Separation Anxiety?

Determining if your dog truly has separation anxiety is the first step. Some dogs are just bored or have not been properly potty trained. **Separation anxiety is a true panic type of response.** A dog may display actions similar to one or more of the following if he has separation anxiety:

- ❑ Barking
- ❑ Howling
- ❑ Pacing
- ❑ Drooling
- ❑ Shaking
- ❑ Elimination
- ❑ Vomiting
- ❑ Self-mutilation
- ❑ Destruction
- ❑ Escape

The best way to determine if your dog has separation anxiety is to set up a video camera so you can record your dog's actions while you are away.

If he exhibits any of the reactions listed above, ask yourself the following questions;

- ▪ Did he seem panicky, or stressed?
- ▪ Was he bored?
- ▪ Did he seem to be having fun?
- ▪ When exactly did the behavior start?

Remember separation is marked by a reaction of stress and panic and those who suffer will usually start to show signs while their owner is getting ready to leave.

Some dogs who are suffering with separation anxiety can have a strong attachment to one particular person so the panic sets in when that one person leaves. The dog with this type of an attachment is not typically comforted by another person; they want their one specific person. Another type of attachment would be the dog who just wants company, they are more concerned with the companionship factor rather than being with one specific person; they just don't want to be alone.

Beginning Treatment Plan-Level One

If you have determined that your dog suffers from separation anxiety you must take action to relieve your dog's distress. This is not a condition to take lightly. Dogs can have a full blown panic attack and suffer severe terror during your departure. To allow this to continue is inhumane.

Treating separation anxiety is about teaching your dog to tap into new emotions when left alone that will alleviate their anxiety. It is not about teaching him **not to** but rather **how to** feel. Our goal is to give them a sense of being relaxed, safe, and happy - yes, happy that you are leaving. This is not a behavior that can be cured quickly, as a matter of fact; it can be a long, tedious challenge. Working alongside a professional, particularly in the beginning stage, is highly recommended.

Step One-*Breaking the cycle of anxiety*

This step is crucial in a successful treatment plan. Remember, you cannot treat your dog's anxiety if he is in a constant state of fear when you leave. If he experiences the cycle of stress and anxiety at any level, you will not be able to treat his condition.

No Intolerable Alone Time - This is when treatment can become tricky. Your dog cannot be alone if he cannot tolerate this experience. This is a necessary step for the treatment plan to be successful. Fortunately, it will be a temporary step until your dog can get over the hump of being alone.

Sit down with your family and have everyone review their schedules to look for ways that will allow someone to be home at all times with your dog during the beginning stages of this process. Be creative in your scheduling, can someone take a different shift at work, or maybe adjust their departure time to fill in missing time gaps? Once your immediate family's schedule is manipulated to the best of your ability, try looking outside for help.

- ❏ Pet sitters
- ❏ Dog day care
- ❏ College students, (Preferably in an animal program)
- ❏ Neighbors
- ❏ Families of your children's friends
- ❏ Church or local clubs
- ❏ Relatives
- ❏ Taking your dog to work

This is not a time to be shy. Your dog is depending on you to help alleviate his panic attacks so it's imperative that you find a solution. You might be surprised at how many people will come to your assistance if you ask, try explaining in detail the exact situation and how devastating it is to your family. Depending on the situation your dog may be able to go to a friend's house vs them coming to yours, this might make it easier for someone to say yes. Offer to trade services or pay for their time, gas or expenses.

Prescription Anti-Anxiety Medication - The use of prescription anti-anxiety drugs may be a necessity for your dog. Some dogs are in such extreme distress that even the slightest distance from their human can put them in a whirlwind of stress. The right medication can help alleviate the panic your dog is feeling, allowing you to treat the behavior by teaching him new associations with being left alone. The rate of learning is quicker when using medication, particularly in the first few months of treatment. Finding the right drug, or drug combination, that works best for your dog can be tricky at first so it is imperative that you work closely with your veterinarian by keeping him updated on the results for every step of your dog's treatment program.

The decision to medicate your dog should not be taken lightly and *must be used parallel with a treatment program* and *not instead of.* Staying on certain medications long term is less than ideal and can play havoc on your dog's organ functions, this means your veterinarian will want to do a full physical including blood work and urinalysis prior to prescribing a medication. If both you, and your veterinarian, feel your dog is healthy enough for a prescription medication you will likely want to do quarterly blood work up to ensure your dog's body and organs are tolerating the medication. Some of the most common medications used to treat separation anxiety are:

- ❖ FDA Approved For Separation Anxiety-Clomicalm/ Clomipramine; Elavil/Amitriptyline -Tricyclic antidepressants; Reconcile/ Fluoxetine hydrochloride-Selective serotonin reuptake inhibitors
- ❖ Extra Label For Separation Anxiety-Paxil/ Paroxetine-SSRI; Xanax /Alprazolam- Benzodiazepines; Valium/Diazepam- Benzodiazepines; Inderal/Propranolol -Beta Blockers; Catapries/Clonidine- Acting alpha-agonist hypotensive agents; Buspirone-Azapirone
- ❖ What **NOT** To Use For Separation Anxiety Acepromazine-Dogs are sedated when on acepromazine, but their brain is still going and functioning and increases stress, and heightens sensitivity to noise.

Over The Counter Anti-Anxiety Options - One common misconception about treating your dog with over the counter remedies is that they are always safe, in reality this is not always true. If you opt to try an over the counter aid, it is still advisable to speak with your veterinarian about proper dosing and possible drug interactions with other medications your dog may be taking. If your veterinarian is unfamiliar with the below list, you can check with a holistic veterinarian who may be more familiar with these options. Visit our resources section on how to locate a qualified holistic veterinarian.

- ❖ Shen Calmer; Botanical Animal-Independence; Botanical Animal-Panic Attack; Homeopet Anxiety Relief, RX Vitamins-NutriCalm; Buck Mountain Botanicals-Valerian; Bach Rescue Remedy; Calcarea phosphorica/ Calcium Phosphate

Additional Calming Aids - Anything that can be added to your dog's daily life to help elevate his stress will prove to be beneficial. The success of your dog's treatment depends on him being stress-free and relaxed. I will give you suggestions on the items and their use as we move through the treatment plan.

- ❖ Through A Dog's Ear; Recorded House Noise; Adaptil (DAP-Dog Appeasing Pheromone); Thunder Shirt; Your Shirt; Ear Plugs (if associated with noise phobia), Acupuncture and Massage

Be Positive - Positive dog training is always the way to go and this is particularly crucial when you are working with a dog who has anxiety issues. Positive reinforcement is a tool used to reinforce good behavior and eliminate undesirable behavior. This approach builds **self-esteem** and inspires **confidence** in your dog.

Dogs' feelings of esteem are very highly influenced by their interaction and relationship with their owners. All dogs need to feel loved and accepted, these feelings can be communicated to your dogs by the way you respond to them. You will be working at building confidence in your dog so stay positive and be careful that you don't take out your frustrations on the dog or allow him to see you angry. Dogs are very sensitive to human emotions and can pick up on our moods faster than we do at times, so it's important to constantly check your emotions to assure they are happy and positive.

Shen Disturbance - Traditional Chinese Medicine has been around for thousands of years. According their philosophy, when a dog has a panicky personality, full of stress and anxiety, he would be considered to have a Shen Disturbance[2]. The Heart Shen allows the dog to be calm and relaxed, something these dogs cannot do. Treatment would include nourishing, or calming the Shen, to aid in their ability to relax and cope.

High Quality Appropriate Diet - I am sure you have heard the old saying, *you are what you eat,* this holds true for our dogs too. Having a proper diet and nutrients is essential for their physical, emotional and mental health. For dogs with Shen disturbances, a cooling diet that contains duck, rabbit, or cod can be very helpful. A neutral diet such as beef or pork will also work. Some other foods that help balance your dog's nervous energy include: sardines, sweet potatoes, chicken eggs, seaweed, kelp, apples and spinach. A tailored diet that is home cooked is the ideal approach to assure your ingredients are from pure, wholesome food sources.

❖ Acupuncture

- ❖ Shen Calmer
- ❖ Cooling Diet
  (Rabbit, duck, cod, blueberries, eggplant, barley, brown rice, wild rice)
- ❖ Leafy Greens, Chicken Eggs, Sardines, Sweet Potatoes, Seaweed or Kelp, Apples and Hearts

Step Two-*Confinement area*

Your confinement area does not have to be the end place you want to leave your dog. This area should be comfortable and ideally in a central part of the house, somewhere you can comfortably stay during training and most importantly, a place your dog can enjoy and relax. This will be the area you spend most of your training in so make sure you think carefully about the location. Choosing a place where your dog can have a view of the exit and/or entrance to your house (front door, garage etc.) would be ideal.

Once you have decided on a suitable and comfortable location you will next need to prep the room. This is where you will start to make the room as cozy as possible and set up some of your additional calming aids.

- ❑ Add various sleeping and resting items such as dog beds, comforters, open dog crate or dog mats. Setting up more than one resting area is ideal and will benefit both your family and your dog.

- ❑ Set up a background noise system that can play CDs such as "Through a Dog's Ear", white noise, or a prerecorded household activity.

- ❑ Plug in the Adaptil/DAP.

- ❑ Provide a basket of safe dog toys and favorite chews.
- ❑ Close the blinds or curtains.
- ❑ Set up a baby gate across the doorway of the confinement room so you can keep your dog in the room without needing to close the door. This will also allow him to see you and that you have clear access to be able to provide treats as needed during training.
- ❑ Set up a video device for recording your dog during your training exercises.
- ❑ Set up a spot inside his containment area where you can spend time with him while you are doing other activities such as watching TV, working on the computer, or reading a book.

Step Three - *Motivation*

Motivation is the first key in a good treatment plan. If your dog is not motivated enough to learn something new, no training will occur. A good motivator is something your dog finds exceptionally valuable. For most dogs, cooked meat, or dehydrated meat are good choices, keep in mind that your dog makes this choice, not you. Try out a few things to see what food gets your dog doing their happy dance or flip-flops.

When using food in dog training, it is important to maintain your dog's daily food calories; you don't want to increase his calorie intake. If you are home cooking for your dog it simplifies things by allowing you to remove some of the meat from his meals to be used when giving him rewards. If you are using dry dog food or another form of feeding, substitute a portion of his daily calories with meat calories.

Step Four - Interactive treat toys

If you have tried to address your dog's separation anxiety in the past, you may have tried to use interactive treat dispensing toys. Unfortunately, a lot of times when a dog is in distress his appetite will shut down so he may lose all interest in food. It is also possible that once he finished eating his treat toys the panic mode set in because the treat toy was empty. Later in this program, we will re-visit this idea and the solution in more gradual steps. First, you must teach your dog how to interact with a stuffed treat toy.

Stuffing A Hollow Chew Toy - Teaching your dog how to use a treat toy might take a little bit of time and patience but in the end, it is well worth the effort. During this phase, you are not teaching your dog how to use the toy in his confinement area, but rather in a location he is already comfortable being in.

1) Start with something wet like canned dog food, organic peanut or almond butter will also work; simply smudge it on the outside of the toy. You want to make it easy enough for your dog to want to interact with the treat toy. Before moving to step two, you want your dog to eagerly lick the toy so this step may take a few days.

2) Once he is eagerly licking the treat off of the outside of the toy the next step is to smudge the wet food into the opening of the toy. The goal is to get him to lick inside the toy for his reward. Again, do not move to the next step until he is easily removing the food from the toy.

3) If you are home cooking or using high-quality canned dog food simply place a 2 or 3 spoonful's inside the treat toy. Set the food filled toy down in front of your dog and let him enjoy as he figures out this new challenge.

➤ If you are using dry dog food, place about 1/4 to 1/8 cup of the dry food in a bowl and add about 2 tablespoons of canned dog food. Stir and mix together so that the dry kibbles are coated with the canned dog food. Place the finished mixture inside the toy and give the stuffed toy to your dog to enjoy.

4) When he has mastered step 3, it is time to increase the challenge level with the stuffed toy. Double your food mixture and place 1/2 the mixture inside the toy, then place the food stuffed toy into the freezer. (Refrigerate the other ½ of this mixture as needed). Once the stuffed treat toy is frozen, remove the toy from the freezer and stuff the remaining mixture on top of the frozen mixture then present the filled toy to your dog. Your dog will be able to enjoy the unfrozen part immediately as the bottom half starts to thaw slowly. The frozen mixture will be quite challenging to master, which will keep your dog busy longer.

5) Once step 4 is mastered, place the entire food mixture inside the hollow toy and freeze. Once the toy and food inside is frozen, remove and feed to your dog. This should keep your dog busy from anywhere between 10 minutes to 35 minutes.

Tip - If your dog leaves the toy and is not interested, it typically means the food inside is not valuable enough, or the challenge is too difficult. Increase the value, and decrease the difficulty. Most of these hollow dog toys are dishwasher safe (top shelf). But I prefer to use cool water and a baby bottle scrubber to clean because I do not like the rubber material to get hot.

Step Five - *In view confinement training*

Now that you have your dog's new confinement area all prepped, it is time to start the desensitizing and counter conditioning process. This is where you start to teach your dog that it is OK to be in his safe room and that it's actually a very enjoyable place.

It is very important that you remember to go slow at all times; this will prevent your dog from getting anxious or panicked. If he seems upset or shows signs of stress, it means that you are moving too quickly. This is the foundation of your work so you want your dog to be able to successfully master this step before moving on to the next one. The more time and practice sessions you put into your dog's training program, the faster and more reliable the final outcome will be.

Practice these sessions when you have 15-45 minutes to spend on the routine.

1) Prepare your dog's stuffed treat toy.

2) Prepare and use any calming aids you plan on using such as Through A Dog's Ear, Thundershirt or Adaptil/DAP.

3) Walk into the confinement area and ask your dog to come in with you. If this is challenging for him, reward him with a high value treat for entering the area. After you are both in the confinement area, close and secure the baby gate.

4) Hand your dog his stuffed treat toy then sit down and start your own activity. You are not going to pay much attention to your dog, just let him do his own thing. After about 5 minutes of your dog chewing his toy, nonchalantly step out of the gated area, close the gate behind you, open the gate and step back into the room and return to the

23

place you were previously sitting. Repeat this sequence about 2-3 times depending on the total length of your practice session.

> ➤ If your dog finds this challenging and cannot relax or eat his stuffed toy, stay in the room for about 15 minutes then casually leave, allowing your dog to follow. Repeat this process until your dog can relax while in the room, then start step 5.

5) When your dog is comfortable with this process, change up the times when you leave the area. So instead of leaving 5 minutes after you have given his stuffed to or chew, sometimes leave immediately after the chew, or 10 minutes after.

6) After your 15-45 minute practice session, turn off your music and both you and your dog quietly leave the confinement area. It is ideal to keep the baby gate open between sessions so your dog can return to this area at his own will.

You will be repeating these steps over several days to a few weeks depending on your dog's anxiety level. Once again, you want your dog to be relaxed during these sessions.

Increasing Step 4 - You will be increasing step 4 until you can be out of the room, but *IN SIGHT for 30 minutes.* When you start to increase the time on the outside of the gate, you can walk casually to different parts of the house as long as they are in sight. Increasing time should go very slow, even 2 seconds at a time. Again, it's important to be constantly evaluating your dog's response and stress levels. As you increase the number of times that you leave the area, try not to always increase the time increments. Sometimes do 2 seconds, 10 seconds, 1 second, 3 seconds etc.

Step Six - *Teaching a station or go to bed*

A lot of dogs who suffer from separation anxiety are overly attached to their humans. If someone gets up for a moment, they may feel the urge to follow. The dog can become anxious if they aren't allowed to follow, cannot follow or they get separated by a shut door (think bathrooms). These dog needs to learn that it is OK for you to step away for them for a moment.

Therefore, the next behavior you will be teaching your dog is to go to a specific location such as his bed or dog mat. This new behavior will be taught slowly and once your dog understands what you are asking him to do, we will pair his station with a stay behavior which you will be able to use instead of allowing him to follow you everywhere.

1) Place a special rug, dog mat, or pet blanket on the floor. This "station" should be portable so that you can use it in different locations. You can even purchase a few and strategically place them in various parts of the house.

2) Take a treat and place it next to your dog's nose and lure him to take a step on the station. Once he does say "**YES!**" and quickly give him the treat. Toss the second treat away from the station so your dog gets off the station to get the treat. Lure your dog back onto the station and repeat the process of treating him on his station and then tossing the second treat off the station. Repeat the lure and treat process, and tossing the second treat away 5 times.

3) Repeat step 2, this time ask him, or lure him to a lay down position on the station. When he does say "**YES!**" and quickly give him the treat. Toss the second treat away from the station so your dog gets off the station. Repeat this step 5 times again.

4) Repeat step 3, this time, say your station cue (such as "Mat" "Bed" or "Station") right before the luring process. When he steps back on the station say "**YES!**" and quickly give him the treat. Toss the second treat away from the station so your dog gets off the mat. Repeat this step 5 times again.

5) Repeat step 4, this time, you are a couple of steps away from the station when you ask and lure. It would look something like this: Standing 3 steps away from the mat, "Bed" lure to bed, lure to a down, "**YES!**" treat, then treat toss.

6) Build step 5 until you can do this about 5 feet away from the mat.

   ➢ Step 1-6 will likely take place over a few days to a week depending on how much time you put into it.

   ➢ Practice your dog's station training in various locations throughout the house, including the confinement area.

Step Seven - *Teaching a stay*

The stay behavior is tied in with your dog's station training. If you remember from the beginning of this booklet, you should only use positive, confidence boosting training methods. The following technique is an excellent way to build a reliable and relaxed stay. Practice the steps in various rooms and locations including your dog's confinement area and on his mat or bed.

1) Start with your dog in a sitting position. After every second, give your dog a treat. After you have given your dog five treats (5 seconds) say "OK" or "All Done" and encourage your dog to get up. Do not make a big fuss on the getting up part; the sitting/staying step is what you will want to focus on. Repeat 5 times.

   ➢ If your dog is successfully sitting/staying, without getting up for the five treats in step 1 increase to two seconds before giving your dog his reward. In other words, he sits for two seconds, receives a treat, continues sitting for another 2 seconds, another treat, receiving 5 treats in total. Repeat for five sets again before giving him his "OK" or "All Done" cue.

   ➢ You will build this stay one second at a time until your dog can master 5 seconds, 5 repetitions. Once this happens, say your stay cue first. So it will go like this: Your dog sits, you say "Stay" count to five, treat, count to five, treat, count to five, treat, count to five, treat, count to five, treat, say "OK" or "All Done" and encourage your dog to get up.

   ➢ If your dog gets up before giving him your release cue, calmly lure him back to his sit position. Do not reprimand him, or tell him "No". If he continues to get up this means the time is too long and the task is too difficult. Decrease his time, in order for him to be successful, even if it's 2 seconds. You want him to be successful.

2) Repeat the above sequence in your dog's lay down position in increments of 1 second until he is able to master 5 seconds.

3) Once you have added your stay cue and have a 5 second sit and down stay, you will continue to increase the time he is in a stay. Keep with the theme of adding 1 second at a time and doing 5 sets before adding more time. So 6 seconds, five sets, 7 seconds, five sets etc. ***Your goal is a "one minute sit and down stay".*** I do not typically recommend doing much more than one minute in a sit stay since it takes more muscle control to hold that position.

After your dog can do a minute stay, it is time to work on distance, or moving away from your dog. So now we are going to focus on steps away, not seconds.

1) Start with your dog in a sitting position. Give him his stay cue, take one small step back then return to your dog and give him a treat. Repeat this five times, giving your dog a treat after every step away and return. After your five sets say "OK" or "All done" and encourage your dog to get up.

   ➤ If your dog cannot hold his sit position when you take a step back, make it easier by only moving one foot slightly back, return your foot and treat. Again, you want to find the balance so your dog can be successful.

2) Continue your distance training by adding one step at a time. Instead of one step back and return and treat, take two steps back, return and treat. Do 5 sets at each level before adding an additional step. ***Your goal is to be able to go 5' away from your dog before returning.***

➢ Remember if at any time your dog is not successful, take fewer steps. You want him to build confidence and be successful so do not, under any circumstances, reprimand him.

➢ Teach your dog how to do this in both the sit and down position.

After your dog can do a 5' stay, it's time to work on the out of sight stay.

3) Start in a location close to an inside door or room partition, this way you can have your dog sit and you can duck behind the divider or door without moving too far away.

4) Start with your dog in a sitting position. Give him his stay cue, take one small step behind the divider then return to your dog and give him a treat. Repeat this five times, giving your dog a treat every time you return from taking a step behind your divider.

5) After your five sets say "OK" or "All done" and encourage your dog to get up.

➢ Build on this behavior by adding on to the time spent behind the divider. Instead of immediately returning, add one second behind the divider before returning. Repeat for 5 sets. Then add two seconds, three seconds, etc.

Your goal is to be able to stay behind the divider for 30 seconds before returning.

➢ Repeat this sequence with your dog in the down position.

Step Eight - *Not being clingy*

Throughout your dog's training sessions in this book, your lessons are focused on teaching your dog to feel confident even if you aren't by his side. This cannot be done without mastering the next step. It is very important to discourage him from being clingy or overly dramatic with you. This is not to be confused with normal bonding; I am not asking you to stop loving, petting or cuddling your dog. On the contrary, I completely encourage this because bonding is imperative for any training to be successful. The difference for this step is that you are going to give him attention on your terms and not when he is demanding it.

Appropriate Attention - From this point forward, you want to make sure you are not rewarding clingy or overly excited attention. Instead, pay attention to your dog often but only when he is calm and relaxed. As a matter of fact, ***increase the attention*** you give your dog, but do it only when you want to, not when he is being demanding. This goes for your greeting behaviors too. When you come home, or when you see your dog after an absence, make the greeting boring and uneventful. If your dog is overly excited, just ignore him until he is more relaxed. Do not reprimand him; just do not pay attention to demanding or exuberant behavior.

Tether System - Tethering is when you take your dog's leash and attache it to a sturdy piece of furniture like the sofa. Ideally these will be extra leashes that are always attached to specific places with easy access to you and your dog. This allows you to be able to quickly hook up your dog so he is secured to one spot while you step into another room without him being able to follow you.

1) Practice tethering your dog *in sight but out of reach* when you do various household activities such as eating, watching TV or doing computer work.

 > You can provide your dog with a stuffed chew toy or chew bone during these lessons.

 > You can also practice your stay exercises during this time.

 > You should NEVER leave your dog unattended while attached to a tether; he could easily wrap himself up and even strangle himself if unsupervised.

Step Nine - *Desensitizing leaving cues and triggers*

Dogs that suffer from separation anxiety are very in tune to the actions we take leading up to our departure. Some dogs are so worried that they focus on things like your alarm. They know that during the week if the alarm goes off this means you will be leaving the house, but on the weekends when there is no alarm it means you will be staying home. This next step focuses on desensitize them to specific activities that they associate with you leaving. Practice these exercises at various times of the day, *but not within 2 hours of a real departure.*

1) Think about your leaving routine. What things do you do before you leave the house? Put your makeup on, work shoes vs. weekend shoes, pick up your keys, open garage door, pack a lunch etc. Determine all your dog's triggers and write them down on a list.

2) Provide your dog with something incredibly tasty and valuable. This may be a good time to use the easy, not

frozen, stuffed treat toy. The reward/food inside the toy should be super valuable to him. Once he's readily chewing on the toy go through the actions from **one** of the triggers on your list, like putting on your coat or picking up your keys. Next, just hang out for about 5 minutes with that trigger on, or in your hands.

> ➤ Repeat this lesson randomly throughout the day with different items. Again, never closer than a couple of hours before a real departure.

> ➤ Once you know your dog can handle these steps without anxiety, move to step 3.

3) This time, start with a trigger FIRST. In other words, pick up your keys, THEN give your dog his food toy, then hang out for five minutes.

> ➤ Repeat this lesson randomly throughout the day with different items. Again, never closer than a couple of hours before a real departure.

> ➤ Once you know your dog can handle these steps without anxiety, move to step 4.

4) This time, add more than one trigger at a time. An example would be to put on your work shoes and coat, then give your dog his food toy and hang out for five minutes.

> ➤ Repeat this lesson randomly throughout the day with different items and sequences. Again, never less than a couple of hours before a real departure.

Step Ten - *Exercise, activities and confidence building*

When a dog acts out and exhibits behavioral problems, increasing the dog's activity is a must. It is much easier to alleviate some of his pent up energy in a more appropriate way. If your dog has plenty of appropriate physical and mental activities, this will aid in his treatment. *It is not a cure, but an aid.*

Daily Activities

- 30 minutes of aerobic activity such as swimming, ball play or light jogging.

- 20-60 minute walk or outing.

- Interactive food puzzle toys (can be combined with your previous lessons).

- (2) 10-15 minute trick training lessons.

- 10-15 minute physical bonding time such as grooming, massage, belly rubs and talking.

- (2) 5 minute challenging games such as find the toy or find the treats.

  ➢ I do not recommend doing physical exercise right before a departure, please allow at least 30 minutes rest time before leaving.

  ➢ Please check with your veterinarian to ensure your dog can endure the activities then edit them if needed to something your dog can safely do.

Confidence building is actually taking place with all of your lessons throughout this book. A dog that lacks confidence typically develops behavioral problems such as separation anxiety. Below are a few ideas and games to help build up your dog's confidence and self-esteem.

33

- ❏ **Tricks**-One of the best benefits of teaching your dog tricks is that it builds your dog's self-confidence and your relationship with your dog. He will learn how to go outside his comfort level by trying something new and being rewarded for it. You can visit my YouTube channel for some ideas at: www.youtube.com/user/toledodogtraining "Dog Tricks"

- ❏ **Find The Toy** - Start by playing with one of your dog's favorite toys. Get a nice game going then ask him to Sit/Stay (or hold him back if he does not know how), and place the toy 5' from him and say, "Find It!" Once he grabs it, start playing again. Eventually, start placing the toy in more difficult places, so that he actually starts to look for it.

- ❏ **Toy Challenge** - Grab one of your dog's favorite toys (or food treat if needed) and toss it under a blanket on the floor with just a part of the toy sticking out. Encourage your dog to get it then make a big fuss when he does. Build on this behavior until the toy is totally covered by the blanket, and finally try wrapping the blanket around the toy a few times.

- ❏ **Obstacles** - Set up different obstacles for your dog to navigate. A broomstick on the floor to walk over, then elevate so he can jump over it (just a few inches high), or maybe a box for him to climb inside, these all make fun obstacles for your dog to learn. Help him navigate around them with treats and encouragement.

- ❏ **Training** - Enroll in a positive dog training class.

Step Eleven - *Relaxation*

Remember, dogs with separation anxiety tend to be on edge so teaching them how to relax is crucial. These relaxation techniques are designed to teach your dog self-control. If practiced on a regular basis, your dog will learn how to stay still for extended periods of time. Teaching this technique takes time and patience, but the rewards, in the end, are priceless.

1) Begin in a quiet location of your house and on a soft surface. Make sure you are going to be distraction-free.

2) Get yourself a comfortable cushion to sit on and maybe turn on your favorite TV program or some relaxing music. Position your dog so that he is close to your body and slowly start to rub his chest in a steady, circular motion.

3) Calmly rub his entire body starting at the base of his head and working your way down to his tail and feet. You may want to speak soothingly to your dog. Try to make it enjoyable to yourself also; if you are in a calm and relaxed state your dog will reflect your peaceful mood.

4) After a few minutes, calmly release your dog. Make sure he is relaxed prior to releasing him. Over time, you can steadily increase the duration your dog is sitting calmly with you.

   ➤ As he progresses, try this technique during more distracting times such as when guests are over, or at the park.

Graduating From Level 1

By the time you move to level 2 your dog should have mastered the following behaviors.

- ❏ Understands how to empty a stuffed treat toy
- ❏ Can be in his confinement area for 30 minutes alone while you are in view
- ❏ Can go to his station while 5' away
- ❏ Can do a one minute sit and down stay
- ❏ Can do a sit and down stay from 5' away
- ❏ Can do an out of sight stay for 30 seconds
- ❏ Understands and can use the tether system for various activities
- ❏ Can tolerate 2 or more combined departure triggers
- ❏ Has increased exercise and activities
- ❏ Has learned new games and tricks
- ❏ Can relax for 5 minutes during a relaxation exercise

Level Two

Now that you have laid a good foundation into your dog's training, it is time to add another layer of your treatment plan. In this level you will start to focus on being out of sight from your dog. It is still important to ensure your dog is stress-free during each level. If you are seeing signs of stress (pacing, whining, not eating treat toy etc.) back it up a step or two. Slow and steady.

Technology is the key to this level. Since you will not be in sight of your dog, you will not be able to observe and monitor his stress level. You will want to have a device and application that can show you live what your dog is doing. Look into something like Skype, Facetime, Google Hangout, icam and Presence, Ustream, or Vimeo. This technology is spreading like wildfire so new live streaming video platforms are popping up constantly. I recommend you search the web for "live streaming apps" and I'm sure you will find something that will fit your set up. Position your device so it is pointing at the general area your dog will be.

Step One - *Out of view confinement training*

This step is almost the same as *Step Five - In view confinement training,* except this time you are focusing on out of sight lessons. The setup is the same, and again you do not want your dog to get anxious or panicked. If he seems upset or stressed this means you are moving too quickly.

1) Prepare the same set up as you did in *Step Five - In view confinement training*.

2) Hand your dog his stuffed treat toy then sit down and do your own activities. Do not pay much attention to your dog, just let him do his own thing.

3) After about 5 minutes of your dog chewing his toy, nonchalantly step out of the gated area, close the gate behind you, and go out of sight for a moment, then return, open the gate and step back into the room returning to the place you were previously sitting. Repeat this sequence 2-3 times depending on the total length of your practice session.

> Pay close attention to your video stream to make sure your dog is not anxious when you are out of sight.

> When your dog is comfortable with this process, change the time when you leave. So instead of leaving 5 minutes after you have given him his chew, sometimes leave immediately after the chew, or 10 minutes after.

4) After your 15-45 minute practice session, turn off your music and both you and your dog quietly leave the confinement area. It is ideal to keep the baby gate open between sessions so your dog can return to this area at his own will.

You will be repeating these steps over a span of several days to a few weeks depending on your dog's anxiety level. Once again, you want your dog to be relaxed during these sessions.

Increasing Step 3 - You will be increasing step 3 until you can be out of the room, ***OUT of SIGHT for 30 minutes.*** When you start to increase the time out of sight remember to increase the time in very small increments, even 2 seconds at a time. Again, evaluate your dog's response and stress by watching the video monitor.

➤ As you increase the time, do not always go up with the time span. Sometimes it is 10 seconds, 3 seconds, 7 seconds....

➤ Your live streaming video is your key to determine how well your dog is doing.

Step Two - *Getting out of the house*

This next step needs to go very slowly for most dogs. Once again, set up your live streaming device when you get to the point of going out of the house. The last thing you want to do is put your dog in a panic.

1) Practice these sessions when you have 15-30 minutes to spend on the routine.

2) If your dog can see your exit location from his confinement area, set him up in his area like you typically do with his calming aids and stuffed toy. If he cannot see you leave from his area, he will need a different location. After determining a location he can see you leave, prep the area up with his calming aids, dog bed and treat toy.

3) After you have given him his stuffed treat toy, casually walk ½ way to your exit location then return to his area and go on to do regular inside activities, ignoring your dog. Repeat the process of going towards your exit and returning to him about every 5 minutes until your training time is over.

➤ If walking ½ way to your exit point is too stressful for your dog, only go as far as he can comfortably tolerate.

4) At your next training session you can build on the distance to the exit, always making this training session casual and not acknowledging your dog when you return to his area.

5) Continue building on this routine over the next several days or weeks depending on your dog's response. Take each step very slow. Example-hand on door knob and return; open door and return; open door and hold open for a second and return; open door, step out and return; open door, step out for 2 seconds and return.

Once your dog is at ease with step 5 of you opening the door and stepping out for a moment before returning then it is time for the big door close. This is where your live stream video is a must.

6) Set up your live streaming video.

7) This time, as you step out the door, shut the door behind you, then immediately open the door and return.

8) Continue to slowly build on this step increasing the time behind the shut door by about 5 seconds at a time. Pay close attention to the live stream of your dog so you can evaluate how he is doing, this will enable you to return prior to him getting anxious. You are going to gradually build this duration to *30 minutes outside of the door.*

  ➤ Remember to stagger your time outside the closed door, do not always increase. 10 seconds, 3 seconds, 15 seconds etc.

Step Three - *Continuing foundation work*

It is important that you still work on the other lessons in this booklet. Keep increasing duration and difficulty levels as your dog masters the previous requirements. It is very important that you do not forget about those departure cues; keep working on desensitizing him to them and their routine and patterns. Everything suggested in this treatment plan plays an important role in your dog's desensitization process and confidence building. You do not want to get lax just because you are seeing improvements in your dog's behavior, instead you want to keep going and keep improving on his training.

Level Three

At this level it is time to start putting everything together to really simulate an actual departure. It is imperative that you remember to stay below your dog's threshold and continue using your resources from level one in not allowing your dog intolerable time alone.

Do not forget you still want to work on the other lessons in this booklet. Keep increasing duration and difficulty levels as your dog masters the previous requirements. Particularly do not forget about those departure cues and stays.

Step One - *Getting out of the house adding leaving triggers*

1) Practice these sessions when you have 15-45 minutes to spend on the routine.

2) Same set up as before (location, calming aids, stuffed toys)

3) It is time to prepare to leave. First, follow your normal leaving procedures exactly, put on shoes, coat, and keys. After you are ready, give your dog his filled treat toy, walk ½ ways to your exit location then turn back around, remove what you just put on (shoes, coat etc.) and then simply sit down and relax. Repeat this process about every 5 minutes until your training time is over.

   ➢ If walking ½ way to your exit point is too stressful for your dog, only go as far as he can comfortably tolerate. On the other hand, if it is easy, go further.

4) At your next training session, build on the distance to the door, always making this training session casual, and not acknowledging your dog when returning to his area.

5) Continue building on this routine over the next several days or weeks depending on your dog's response. Take each step very slow just like you did previously. When you get to the point of shutting the door, make sure you lock the door it to mimic your true departure routine. If your exit is through the garage then open and close the garage door (do not leave). Your goal is to be *30 minutes outside of the door.*

   ➢ Remember you are watching your dog through live streaming video to determine when to increase time or decrease time.

Level Four

Now that your dog can easily tolerate being alone for 30 minutes, you should be able to increase the time away from your dog in larger chunks. You will also be adding more triggers into your routine.

Once again, you still must work on the other lessons throughout this this booklet. Keep increasing criteria and add distractions. Departure cues, confidence building games and stays are important.

Step One - *Leaving your house*

1) Practice these sessions when you have from 45 minutes -2 hours to spend on the routine.

2) Same set up as before (location, calming aids, stuffed toys)

3) In this step you are doing all of your normal departure cues but this is the real deal. Remember in *Step One - Getting out of the house adding leaving triggers,* you incorporated all these triggers into your 30 minute departure, so this should be the same. Go out the door or garage (whichever is normal) and start your car. Turn your car off and return to the house, take off all your gear (coat, shoes etc.) then sit down and relax. Repeat this process about every 5 minutes until your training time is over.

   ➤ Slowly increase the time your car is running before returning to the house.

> ➤ Remember you are watching your dog through the live video streaming to ensure he is not stressed.

4) Once your dog can tolerate 1 minute of your car running, drive around the block, then return to the house. Turn your car off, go back inside the house, take off all your gear (coat, shoes etc.) then sit down and relax. Repeat this process about every 5 minutes until your training time is over.

5) At your next training session, build on the distance you drive away making this training session casual and not acknowledging your dog when coming back. Pay close attention to your dog on the live streaming video so that you can accurately build or decrease the time you are gone. ***Your goal is to be gone 4 hours.***

Level Five And Beyond

Step One - *Maintaining*

It is important to continually work with your dog on all the training lessons and games throughout your dog's life. Separation anxiety has a high success rate if following a good treatment plan. It does have the ability to re-occur, particularly after a stressful incident, but if you have successfully gone through this and continue to practice the lessons, you have a good head start to getting through it again.

Some dogs will be able to tolerate one leave a day, but not two. You will likely need to have good planning skills throughout your dog's life.

Believe me, I know treating separation anxiety can be a very daunting, time consuming, and a boring behavior problem to address. But your dog is worth it! His love for you is unconditional and so immense that he is terrified when you leave. He is not misbehaving or trying to be bad, he just cannot function alone. He is counting on you to help him through his trauma. I highly recommend getting a good dog training coach to help guide you through this process and to help you set accurate criteria for your dog and trouble shoot any hiccups you may have.

You got this!

Resources

Throughout this booklet I mentioned various products that can assist you in treating separation anxiety. Instead of naming names in print, I have an ongoing list of recommended products, reviews and articles on my Global Dog Training website under "Shop Now". The reasoning is that manufactures often come and go but there is always new knowledge waiting to be discovered. It pays to keep updated on the latest innovative products. You can avoid wasting time searching the web by visiting my web sites for all the updated dog training articles and tips.

If you need additional help, I offer private training in person or via phone/Skype. Together we will work closely on a treatment plan. I will coach you, troubleshoot problems, and most importantly be there for you emotionally. Don't hesitate to reach out.

My Personal Websites

- www.Globaldogtraining.com
  - Dog training articles and tips
  - Dog training videos
  - Purchase my other books
  - Holistic dog care information
  - Home cooking for your dog
  - Showcasing the best products for your dog
  - Dog product reviews

One on one support and workshops including staff training
Dog trainer referral service

❏ www.Vacationswithyourdog.com
  ➢ Dog friendly destinations, lodging, attractions, shopping and dining
  ➢ Dog travel tips

References

1. Voith, V.L., Borchelt, P.L., 1996. Separation anxiety in dogs. In: Borchelt, P.L. (Ed.), Readings in Companion Animal Behaviour. Veterinary Learning Systems, Trenton, NJ.
2. Morgan, Judy www.Drjudymorgan.com

56750126R00029

Made in the USA
Charleston, SC
30 May 2016